Original title:
Moonlight Melodies and Snuggles



Author: Samuel Kensington

ISBN HARDBACK: 978-9916-90-384-1
ISBN PAPERBACK: 978-9916-90-385-8

## The Gentle Touch of Night's Embrace

The stars awaken in the deep,
As shadows dance and softly creep.
The moon's glow bathes the world in light,
A tender hush, the end of night.

Beneath the sky, the secrets rest,
In whispered tones, the heart feels blessed.
With every sigh, the silence grows,
In night’s embrace, pure comfort flows.

## Celestial Whispers in the Dark

The cosmos sings its velvet tune,
Where dreams take flight beneath the moon.
A melody of starlit grace,
In shadows deep, we find our place.

Each twinkling light, a soft caress,
In cosmic dance, our souls confess.
With every breath the night inspires,
A spark of hope that never tires.

## Silvery Glow of Peaceful Dreams

In quiet realms where silence sleeps,
The silver glow of starlight creeps.
Wrapped in clouds of midnight blue,
Our deepest hopes begin anew.

The whispers of the night unfold,
In dreams we find our hearts consoled.
Each vision clear, a sweet delight,
As peace descends on gentle night.

## Comfort in the Gentle Twilight

As day gives way to dusk's embrace,
The softening light reveals our place.
In twilight's hue, we find our peace,
A moment's pause, a sweet release.

With every breeze, the world slows down,
In quiet grace, we wear our crown.
A tranquil heart, the stars align,
In gentle twilight, our spirits shine.

## Nighttime Serenades and Gentle Breezes

Whispers of the night abound,
Softly through the willows sound.
Moonlight dances on the stream,
Filling hearts with quiet dreams.

Crickets play a lullaby,
Stars above begin to sigh.
Gentle breezes start to play,
Guiding thoughts that drift away.

## Warmth Beneath a Starry Veil

Underneath the velvet sky,
Fireflies flicker as they fly.
Warmth embraced by nature's breath,
A soothing peace that conquers death.

Silhouettes of trees stand tall,
Guardians to the night's sweet call.
Dreams are woven through the night,
In their glow, all feels just right.

## Radiance of a Softly Glowing Hour

In the quiet hour of dusk,
Nature's calm, a fragrant musk.
Colors blend in golden hue,
Painting skies with vibrant blue.

As the world begins to rest,
Hearts will pulse, a gentle quest.
Moonlight spills—a silver stream,
Waking hopes from evening's dream.

## Enchanted Nights of Comfort

Through the dark, the stars emerge,
Guiding souls on paths we verge.
In the night, hearts intertwine,
Comfort found in love's design.

Laughter echoes, sweet and clear,
While the ones we hold most dear.
Magic floats upon the air,
In this night, we are aware.

## Caresses of the Whispering Breeze

Gentle whispers through the trees,
Carrying secrets with the ease.
Each soft touch, a tender sigh,
Lifting dreams that drift on high.

Moonlit shadows dance with grace,
Filling night with warm embrace.
Nature's breath, a soothing balm,
In its presence, all is calm.

## Floating on a Cloud of Quietude

Silken threads of silence weave,
In the stillness, hearts believe.
Drifting gently, time stands still,
Whispers soft, a sweet thrill.

Up above, the world feels light,
Wrapped in dreams, away from night.
Softly spoken, lullabies,
In this peace, our spirit flies.

## Embraced by the Light of Infinity

Stars like lanterns softly burn,
In their glow, the hearts can turn.
Shining bright through endless space,
Each a kiss, a warm embrace.

Time dissolves in cosmic flow,
Guided where the dreamers go.
In the vast, we find our place,
Wrapped in love, a soft embrace.

## Celestial Comforts of the Heart

Softly glowing, twilight skies,
In their beauty, hope will rise.
Every heartbeat sings its part,
In the cosmos, a sweet start.

Whispers echo from above,
Filling souls with endless love.
In the silence, hearts take flight,
Wrapped in warmth, we greet the night.

## Where Dreams and Nightlight Meet

In shadows deep, where whispers play,
The gentle glow lights up the way.
Each thought takes flight, a starry chart,
As night unfolds, it warms the heart.

Beneath the veil of midnight's grace,
We find a home, a sacred space.
With every dream, the world awakes,
In twilight's arms, the spirit breaks.

## Harmonies of Heartfelt Slumber

A lullaby floats through the air,
Soft melodies, without a care.
In dreams we dance on silver beams,
Where hope resides and pure love gleams.

The stars align, a guiding light,
In quiet realms, we drift tonight.
With every beat, our hearts entwine,
In slumber's arms, all souls align.

## Driftwood Dreams in the Glistening Light

On shores of thought, where dreams reside,
Driftwood whispers, the calmest tide.
With every wave, the stories flow,
In glistening light, our spirits grow.

Each grain of sand, a tale to tell,
Of distant lands and time's soft spell.
Together here, we find our flight,
In dreams that shimmer through the night.

## Embracing the Night's Gentle Aura

The night unfolds with tender grace,
An emerald sky, a warm embrace.
With every star, a wish takes flight,
In peaceful dreams, we find our light.

The moon, a guardian up above,
Whispers secrets of gentle love.
As shadows dance, our spirits soar,
In night’s embrace, we crave for more.

## Twilight's Hush of Endearment

The sun dips low, the sky aglow,
Whispers of dusk, in soft shadows flow.
Colors blend in a gentle embrace,
Nature breathes out, in this sacred space.

Stars blink awake, a distant choir,
Moonlight sings of dreams, igniting desire.
In twilight's hush, hearts softly sigh,
Wrapped in warmth, as time drifts by.

## Heartstrings Plucked by Evening's Glow

The day retreats with a golden hand,
Painting the sky, a vision so grand.
Each star appears, a note in a song,
In evening's glow, where we belong.

Love dances lightly on the cool breeze,
Softly it whispers, puts the heart at ease.
With every heartbeat, the night unfolds,
Wrapped in the magic that twilight holds.

## The Lull of the Night's Warmth

In the embrace of night’s gentle hold,
Dreams are woven, like stories untold.
Moonbeams shine, a soothing balm,
Filling the air with a whisper of calm.

Silence sings softly, a cradle of grace,
Stars smile down, in their velvet space.
As shadows dance, we close our eyes,
Beneath the heavens, where comfort lies.

## Floating in the Glow of Serenity

In the stillness, the heart takes flight,
Basking in the glow of a peaceful night.
Moments linger, like leaves in the air,
Floating gently, without a care.

The world fades softly, a distant hum,
In the calm embrace, we feel love's drum.
Serenity wraps us in tender grace,
Guiding our spirits to a tranquil place.

## Secrets in the Sway of the Night

Whispers carried on the breeze,
Secrets hiding in the trees.
Moonlight dances on the ground,
Mysteries in shadows found.

Stars above begin to gleam,
Filling hearts with gentle dreams.
Eerie silence all around,
Nature's whispers softly sound.

Footsteps echo, soft and light,
Chasing thoughts on wings of night.
Breathless moments, time stands still,
Captured by the night’s soft thrill.

## Celestial Cuddles

In the arms of midnight’s hue,
Stars surround me, shining through.
Gentle sighs of a cooling breeze,
Wrapped in warmth, my worries freeze.

Sparkling dreams take flight and soar,
Underneath the sky's great door.
Galaxies whisper tales so sweet,
A cosmic dance, my heart's heartbeat.

Softly cradled by the light,
I find comfort in the night.
Celestial cuddles, deep and wide,
In this vast, enchanting tide.

## Embracing the Night's Serenade

Notes of night weave through the air,
A serenade beyond compare.
Crickets strum their softest song,
Embracing night where dreams belong.

The moon hums low, a lullaby,
Nurtured by the endless sky.
With every chord, my spirit lifts,
In this moment, love's sweet gifts.

Stars join in, a cosmic choir,
Painting wishes, hearts inspired.
Embracing all that feels so right,
Lost within the magic of night.

## Dreaming in the Silvery Glow

Silvery beams through window panes,
Inviting dreams on moonlit trains.
Each thought drifts like clouds afar,
Guided softly by a star.

Nighttime whispers weave and thread,
Tales of wonder, softly spread.
Where imagination starts to flow,
Awakening the heart’s warm glow.

Underneath this shimmering light,
I find solace, pure delight.
Dreaming deep in slumber's hold,
Wrapped in warmth, the night unfolds.

## Tender Moments in Lunar Light

In the hush of night we stand,
Whispers soft like grains of sand.
Beneath a sky of silver hue,
Every heartbeat speaks of you.

Moonbeams dance upon your face,
In this still, enchanted place.
Tender gazes, gentle sighs,
Love reflected in our eyes.

## Twilight's Warm Embrace

As daylight fades to softer dreams,
Colors blend in gentle streams.
Whispers of the day now rest,
In twilight's glow, our hearts are blessed.

The stars awaken, one by one,
A canvas painted by the sun.
Hand in hand, we share a space,
Lost in twilight's warm embrace.

## Driftwood Dreams Under Celestial Light

Upon the shore where driftwood lies,
We gather hopes beneath the skies.
The ocean hums a lullaby,
As dreams take flight, they learn to fly.

Underneath the silver glow,
The tides of time continue slow.
With every wave, a secret shared,
In this embrace, we are prepared.

## Stardust and Silk

In a world of stardust bliss,
Each moment wrapped in tender kiss.
Silken threads of fate entwine,
Creating echoes, yours and mine.

As galaxies above us spin,
Our journey starts, our hearts begin.
With every spark that lights the night,
We weave our dreams in pure delight.

## Tucked Beneath the Cosmic Glow

Stars whisper softly above us,
Wrapped in the night's warm embrace.
Dreams dance like fireflies flickering,
In the vastness of time and space.

Moonlight spills over the hills,
Casting shadows where secrets lie.
Winds carry tales from afar,
As the universe breathes a sigh.

Beneath the cosmic glow we linger,
Hearts beating in rhythmic unison.
Hope shines bright in the stillness,
A beacon for souls almost won.

In this moment, we are timeless,
The world fades into soft night.
Tucked beneath the cosmic glow,
Everything feels just right.

## A Softer Shade of Nightly Bliss

Gentle breezes weave through the trees,
Carrying scents of lavender dreams.
Night unfolds in soft, soothing hues,
Cradling hearts in moonlit beams.

Stars twinkle like notes of music,
Each one a whispered serenade.
Lost in this softer shade of night,
We find peace as worries fade.

Silence wraps us in its comfort,
As shadows dance upon the ground.
In the stillness, love's sweet echo,
Is the only voice that we've found.

A canvas painted with twilight,
Boundless beauty held in our sight.
A softer shade of nightly bliss,
Where dreams take flight, hearts ignite.

## The Embrace of Night's Tranquil Song

Underneath the blanket of night,
Whispers of calm begin to swell.
Each star a note in the silence,
Binding the earth in a spell.

The moon shines bright with a gentle grace,
Illuminating paths of dreams.
In the stillness, we find our place,
As the world fades to soft themes.

Crickets provide a soothing chorus,
Nature’s lullaby fills the air.
Held close in night’s tender embrace,
We breathe deep, forgetting our care.

In this moment, all is right,
Hearts entwined beneath dark skies.
The embrace of night’s tranquil song,
Stirs our souls, ignites our sighs.

## The Soft Embrace of Evening

The sun dips low in the sky,
Casting shadows long and shy.
Colors blend in warm hues,
A peaceful end to the day's dues.

Whispers of wind gently play,
As night prepares to steal the day.
Stars awaken, one by one,
Beneath the moon, the world feels spun.

Crickets sing their twilight songs,
Nature hums, where each heart belongs.
The horizon melts into dreams,
Wrapped in soft, golden beams.

A quiet calm envelops all,
As darkness starts to softly crawl.
The embrace of evening shines,
In hushed moments, love defines.

## Echoes Beneath the Lunar Veil

Moonlight dances on the waves,
Lighting paths where silence saves.
The nightingale sings her tune,
Echoes rise beneath the moon.

Clouds drift softly, shadows play,
Whispers lost in night's ballet.
Stars above like diamonds glow,
As gentle breezes start to flow.

In the hush, time stands still,
Dreams awaken, hearts fulfill.
Underneath the lunar veil,
Stories linger, whispers sail.

A canvas brushed with silver light,
Illuminates the velvet night.
Echoes linger, tales of old,
In the quiet, magic unfolds.

## A Blanket of Gleaming Night

The sky unfolds a cosmic sheet,
Where stars converge and softly meet.
A blanket draped with twinkling fire,
Ignites the heart with pure desire.

Each speck of light, a wish in flight,
Guiding souls through the deep night.
The moon serves as a silver guide,
In the dark, dreams do abide.

Gentle winds whisper secrets near,
Filled with hopes, both bright and clear.
The world beneath is hushed and calm,
Cradled softly, like a psalm.

A blanket soft, wrapped close and tight,
Holding warmth in the cool night.
In its embrace, all fears take flight,
Together in this gleaming light.

## Soft Serenades of Dusk

As daylight fades, a serenade,
Of colors bright that soon invade.
The sky blurs gold, then fades to grey,
In twilight's hush, night finds its way.

Soft notes drift on the cooling air,
Filling hearts, light as a prayer.
The world transforms, a gentle shift,
As nature offers her soft gift.

Birds sing their last, sweet refrain,
In harmony with the soothing rain.
The horizon glows, a fading ember,
In the calm, we remember.

Dusk unfolds its velvet shroud,
Cradling dreams within the crowd.
A serenade for souls in trust,
As day gives way to night's soft rust.

## The Caressing Glow of Evening

The sun dips low in the sky,
Casting hues of orange and pink.
Cool breezes softly sigh,
As day and night begin to link.

Trees sway gently in the breeze,
Whispers of secrets in the air.
Birds trilling sweet melodies,
Soft shadows dance everywhere.

Golden rays kiss the earth,
As twilight begins to unfold.
Moments of beauty and mirth,
Wrapped in stories yet untold.

The world slows down, takes a breath,
Underneath the vast expanse.
Embracing life, dancing with death,
In the evening's tender glance.

## Melodies in the Whispering Night

Moonlight spills across the ground,
A symphony of soft, sweet light.
In the stillness, magic's found,
Melodies weave through the night.

Crickets sing their gentle song,
Notes of nature's serenade.
Echoes linger, soft and long,
As shadows in the dark parade.

Stars twinkle like distant dreams,
Painting a canvas above.
The world is richer than it seems,
Wrapped in the night’s peaceful love.

Every whisper, every sigh,
Carries secrets to the moon.
In this moment, I could fly,
Dancing to the night’s sweet tune.

## The Cradle of Starlit Comfort

In the cradle of the night sky,
Stars twinkle like lullabies.
Holding dreams as they fly,
A gentle hush of tender sighs.

The universe wraps us tight,
In a blanket of shining light.
Silvery beams chase away fright,
Our hearts beat soft, pure delight.

A canvas of dreams unfolds,
In the embrace of endless space.
Stories of time, yet untold,
Swirl gently in this sacred place.

In this serene, starlit dome,
We find comfort, peace, and grace.
It feels, in this moment, like home,
In the galaxy's loving embrace.

## Evening's Gentle Lull

As the sun yields to the night,
A calming hush drapes the land.
Stars awaken, shining bright,
As moonbeams carve the soft sand.

Crickets start their nightly show,
A melody soft and sweet.
The world sways, moving slow,
As dreams gather at our feet.

In this lull, we find our peace,
Wrapped in twilight's tender veil.
A promise that troubles cease,
In every whisper, every tale.

Evening’s sigh brings rest profound,
With every shadow softly cast.
In this magic, love abounds,
As night unfolds, our spirits last.

## Celestial Murmurs in the Stillness

In the night a whisper glows,
Where the silent cosmos flow.
Stars like jewels in velvet skies,
Stirring dreams, where wonder lies.

Gentle breezes soft and light,
Carry secrets of the night.
Each twinkle, a soft embrace,
Wraps the heart in time and space.

## Sighs of Comfort Amidst Twilight

As daylight fades, shadows blend,
Whispers linger, night ascend.
Crickets trill with calming tunes,
Underneath the watchful moons.

A canvas painted deep and wide,
Where dreams and hope will coincide.
The dusk a blanket, warm and near,
Hearts find solace, free from fear.

## Serenades Between the Stars

A lullaby that softly sings,
Drifting on the darkest wings.
In the silence, joy ignites,
Melodies in starry nights.

Each note a wish, a tale retold,
Of love and dreams, both brave and bold.
A symphony of light and grace,
Echoing through time and space.

## Comfort of the Quiet Universe

In the calm, a stillness grows,
Where every heart can find repose.
Galaxies in gentle sway,
Guide the weary on their way.

Softly woven threads of night,
Knit together pure delight.
In this space, our spirits soar,
Finding peace forevermore.

## Stars' Caress on Slumbering Souls

In the silent night, stars gleam bright,
Whispers of dreams take gentle flight.
Moonlight dances on tranquil seas,
Embracing hearts with a tender breeze.

Softly wrapped in a soothing shroud,
Floating on clouds, far from the crowd.
Every twinkle a lullaby's call,
Guiding lost souls through night's gentle fall.

Soft shadows play, in calm embrace,
As the world fades, time finds its pace.
Stars weave stories in velvet skies,
Awakening wonders in sleepy eyes.

Cradled in night's warm, loving arms,
Each heartbeat slows, beneath its charms.
A caress of light on slumbering souls,
Whispers of peace that the night extols.

## Nocturnal Harmonies and Snug Retreats

In hidden nooks, the shadows sigh,
Songs of the night softly drift by.
Crickets chirp in a rhythmic tune,
Beneath the watchful gaze of the moon.

Nestled in blankets, warmth surrounds,
Comfort found in the night's soft sounds.
With every note, worries unwind,
A symphony of peace intertwined.

Stars twinkle bright like distant dreams,
They hold the secrets of quiet streams.
A lullaby played by the wind's soft breath,
Guides us gently through the dance of death.

In these snug retreats where shadows play,
Time drifts slowly, night softly sways.
Moments cherished with hearts aglow,
In nocturnal harmonies, love does flow.

## Embracing the Dusk's Tender Glow

Dusk spills colors across the sky,
Whispers of twilight softly sigh.
Golden hues melt into the night,
Embracing shadows, bringing delight.

The world slows down as day bids adieu,
A gentle embrace as dreams come true.
Stars awaken in the velvet dark,
Igniting hope with their shimmering spark.

Breezes carry scents of night's bloom,
Guiding lost hearts to find their room.
Under the veil of the soft twilight,
Moments of peace, a sweet respite.

Embracing the dusk, we find our place,
Bathed in the warmth of night's tender grace.
In this quiet hour, our spirits soar,
As the night whispers of forevermore.

## The Gentle Drift of Night's Soft Tune

Night unfurls its velvet cloak,
In shadows deep, soft dreams invoke.
A gentle drift through starry skies,
Where solace sings and hope replies.

With every sigh, the world slows down,
A serenade in twilight's crown.
Crickets strum a tender song,
Echoes of love where we belong.

Starlit paths where memories weave,
In the quiet hush, we learn to believe.
A lull of peace in night's embrace,
Whispers of joy, time leaves no trace.

Let the night's tune cradle your soul,
In its soft rhythm, be made whole.
For in this drift of silken light,
We find our dreams take graceful flight.

## Elysian Whispers of the Night

Shadows wrap the earth in silk,
A soft embrace, where dreams are built.
Moonlight weaves through whispered trees,
Carrying secrets on the breeze.

Glimmers dance on tranquil streams,
Evening hums of gentle dreams.
Stars ignite the velvet sea,
Inviting hearts to wander free.

Echoes of the nightingale,
Sing of love, and tales they tell.
In this realm where silence sighs,
Elysian whispers softly rise.

Awake the soul with twilight's touch,
In every breath, we feel so much.
As night unfolds its mystic art,
We find our peace, we find our heart.

## Dreams Born from Starlit Caresses

In the hush of night's embrace,
Dreams unfurl with timeless grace.
Stars above, like diamonds glow,
Kiss the world with softest flow.

Each twinkle tells a story bright,
Whispers drift on wings of light.
Midnight, wrapped in silken air,
Holds the secrets, soft and rare.

With the dawn, the dreams shall fade,
But in the heart, their magic stayed.
Starlit caresses weave and spin,
In the soul, they stir within.

As morning breaks, the shadows play,
And dreams will lead us on our way.
In every sigh of night anew,
Reflects the dreams we ever knew.

## Lullaby for the Mid-Night Dance

Close your eyes, let worries cease,
In the night, we find our peace.
Moonbeams cradle, softly sway,
Join the stars in sweet ballet.

The nightingale sings her tune,
Beneath the watchful silver moon.
Every note a gentle wave,
For restless hearts that yearn and crave.

With each breath, we drift away,
To find our joy in night's display.
Melodies in velvet skies,
Whisper softly, lullabies.

So take my hand, let's spin around,
In the hush, all love is found.
Dance until the morning light,
In this lullaby of night.

## Heart's Embrace Under the Evening Sky

Underneath the painted sky,
Hearts unite as shadows lie.
Crimson hues and twilight's glow,
Wrap us tight as breezes flow.

Each whispered vow, a sacred flame,
In love's embrace, we stake our claim.
As stars alight in cosmic play,
Our souls entwined, we drift away.

Through twilight’s hush, we walk as one,
Feeling warmth from setting sun.
Every glance, a promise made,
In this moment, never fade.

Forever held in sunset’s light,
Two hearts merge beneath the night.
In the skies where dreams take flight,
Together always, hearts ignite.

## Twilight Whispers of Comfort

In the dusk, soft shadows play,
Where the weary find their way.
Gentle breezes, secrets shared,
Whispers of love, silently bared.

Stars awaken, their glow so bright,
Guiding dreams into the night.
Moonlight weaves a silver thread,
Wrapping hearts in warmth, widespread.

Nature hums a soothing tune,
Beneath the watchful, gentle moon.
Echoes of hope fill the air,
In this stillness, we lay bare.

Find your solace in the calm,
Let the twilight be your balm.
In the hush of fading light,
Comfort cradles you tonight.

## Whispers of the Night

The moon spills silver on the ground,
While constellations dance around.
Each star a story, softly told,
In the darkness, dreams unfold.

Beneath the veil of night's embrace,
Time slows down, a tranquil pace.
Whispers linger in the air,
Promises of peace everywhere.

A gentle breeze begins to sigh,
Carrying secrets from the sky.
Rest your thoughts, let worries cease,
In the quiet, find your peace.

Nighttime holds a mystic grace,
Illuminating every face.
For in this calm, we can ignite,
The whispers of the endless night.

## Lullabies in Silver Hues

Underneath the silver glow,
Lullabies begin to flow.
Softly sung by night's own choir,
Filling hearts with sweet desire.

Crickets play their serenade,
In the cool, inviting shade.
Each note dances on the breeze,
Bringing warmth and gentle ease.

Starlit skies, a sight so rare,
Wrapped in dreams, we shed our care.
In the fabric of the night,
Lullabies cradle us so tight.

Gaze upon the heavens wide,
Let your inner fears subside.
In these moments, pure and true,
Silver hues will comfort you.

## Embrace of the Starlit Sky

The starlit sky, a quilt of dreams,
Where hope and wonder softly gleam.
Stars like diamonds, bright and vast,
Whisper tales of futures cast.

Wrapped in night's gentle embrace,
Every shadow finds its place.
In the silence, hearts align,
Finding solace, so divine.

Clouds drift by like thoughts unspooled,
In this moment, we are fueled.
Breathe in deep the night's sweet air,
Let worries go, shed every care.

Embrace the magic, hold it tight,
In the arms of the soft night light.
For beneath the stars so high,
We discover dreams that never die.

## Silken Shadows and Sweet Dreams

In the quiet night, silken shadows play,
Whispers of dreams that silently sway.
They weave through the dark, with grace they glide,
Carrying secrets, where hopes abide.

Stars twinkle softly, a lullaby's charm,
Wrapped in the night, we feel their calm.
The world outside fades, in slumber we drift,
In the arms of sweet dreams, our spirits lift.

Moonlight glimmers on the night's cool face,
Illuminating dreams in a tender embrace.
Each moment a gem, in silence it gleams,
In the heart of the dark, we find our dreams.

## Rhythms of the Night's Embrace

The night unfolds, a rhythmic delight,
Whispers of shadows, cloaked in the night.
Every heartbeat echoes, a soft serenade,
In the still, we find the dreams that we made.

Stars compose songs, a celestial choir,
Flickering flames, igniting desire.
Beneath the dark blanket, mysteries sleep,
In the rhythm of night, our secrets we keep.

Winds carry tales from afar and wide,
Through shadows they swirl, our hearts open wide.
Embraced by the calm, we surrender our fears,
To the rhythms of night, woven through years.

## Gentle Caress of Nightfall

Nightfall descends with a gentle caress,
Whispers of silence, a tender finesse.
Stars twinkle brightly, like dreams from afar,
Guiding our hearts like a well-tuned guitar.

In the softening dusk, we find our reprieve,
Lost in the moments, a web we believe.
Moonbeams weave stories in shadows' embrace,
Painting our visions on the evening's face.

Laughter fades softly as twilight draws near,
With each gentle breath, the night's pulse we hear.
Wrapped in the stillness, our souls intertwine,
In the gentle caress, we feel the divine.

## The Harmonious Dance of Shadows

Shadows dance lightly, in a waltz of the night,
Echoes of whispers, soft and polite.
They twirl and they spin, in the pale moon's glow,
Weaving a tapestry, a mystical show.

Each flicker and flutter, a story unfolds,
In the arms of the darkness, a magic that holds.
Dreams intertwine like the stars in the sky,
In the harmonious dance, our spirits fly high.

Underneath the watchful gaze of the moon,
Shadows find solace in their gentle tune.
With every beat, they align with our hearts,
In the dance of the night, a world that imparts.

## Dreamy Wishes Under Celestial Canopy

Beneath the stars, our hopes take flight,
Whispers of dreams in the quiet night.
Softly we drift on the moonlit sea,
Holding our wishes, just you and me.

A gentle breeze carries secrets afar,
Painting the darkness with each glowing star.
In the embrace of the velvet sky,
We make our promises, as time slips by.

With every twinkle, a dream takes shape,
Crafting new worlds, each a wondrous escape.
In hushed tones, we share our delight,
Wrapped in the magic of this serene night.

So let our hearts be open and true,
In this enchanted space, just me and you.
As wishes abound, we'll rise and soar,
Under the canopy, forevermore.

## A Serenade for Cozy Hearts

In the corner, softly glow the lights,
Flickering gently through the cozy nights.
Under blankets, we find our warm place,
Wrapped in the love that time cannot erase.

Melodies whisper like leaves in the breeze,
A loving tune that puts our hearts at ease.
With every note, we sway and unwind,
Creating a haven, a sanctuary defined.

The world outside fades, a distant dream,
In this cocoon, love is the only theme.
Together we laugh, together we sigh,
In the embrace of our sweet lullaby.

So take my hand as we dance through the dark,
With every heartbeat, we find our spark.
In this serenade, our souls take flight,
Cozy and warm in the stillness of night.

## Light and Lullabies Amidst the Stars

The night unfolds, a canvas of light,
Lullabies cradle the world within sight.
Stars are the notes in this cosmic tune,
Singing us softly beneath the bright moon.

With every twinkle, dreams weave and play,
Guiding our hearts in a beautiful way.
The sky is alive with secrets to share,
Each glittering gem, a wish in midair.

As night deepens, our worries take flight,
Floating like feathers on the breeze of the night.
We'll gather our thoughts and take to the skies,
With light as our guide, where the heart never lies.

So hold my hand and let's drift away,
To the realm of dreams where we long to stay.
In light and lullabies, we'll find our peace,
Together forever, as worries release.

## Night's Embrace by the Fireside

Embers dance with a whispering glow,
Casting soft shadows as night starts to flow.
By the fireside, stories weave tight,
In the warm embrace of this tranquil night.

The crackling logs sing a soothing song,
Where moments linger and dreams belong.
With every flicker, our hopes come alive,
In the heart of the night, our spirits thrive.

Wrapped in warmth, we let time stand still,
Sharing our thoughts, a magical thrill.
As the firelight flickers, our hearts align,
In this sacred space, your hand in mine.

So here's to the night, a gentle reprieve,
Together, my love, in dreams we believe.
As the world sleeps soundly, we'll remain awake,
By the fireside's glow, our memories we'll make.

## Cozy Embraces Under Celestial Beams

Wrapped in warmth, we find our place,
Soft shadows dance, a sweet embrace.
Beneath the stars that shimmer and gleam,
We share our thoughts, like a cherished dream.

The night unfolds with tender grace,
As whispers mingle, hearts interlace.
The moonlight bathes us in its glow,
In this quiet moment, love starts to flow.

Crickets sing a lullaby so sweet,
Each gentle breath feels like a treat.
With every heartbeat, our souls entwine,
In this serene world, all feels divine.

Together we cherish this calm delight,
Cozy embraces through the night.
Under celestial beams, we stay,
In this magical realm, we drift away.

## Starlit Comforts

Under a sky of twinkling lights,
We find our solace in starry nights.
A blanket woven from dreams so bright,
Cocooned in comfort, hearts take flight.

The world fades away, just you and me,
In softest stillness, we feel so free.
With every glance, we touch the sky,
In starlit comforts, we learn to fly.

The whispers of the universe call,
In this quiet space, we have it all.
Each shared laugh, a spark in the dark,
Guided by love, we leave our mark.

As constellations dance above our heads,
We weave our stories, where magic spreads.
Together we bask in the cosmic glow,
With starlit comforts, our spirits grow.

## Harmonies in the Midnight Air

In the hush of night, melodies play,
Soft serenades, keep fears at bay.
A gentle breeze carries sweet refrain,
Harmonies linger, like soft summer rain.

The moonlight weaves its silvery thread,
With every note, our spirits are fed.
In whispered songs that the shadows share,
We find our peace in the midnight air.

Dancing fireflies illuminate the scene,
Each flicker a signal, a secret unseen.
As laughter echoes through the reaches of night,
Harmonies guide us, souls take flight.

Together we sway to the rhythm of time,
In this dusk-lit moment, all feels sublime.
With music wrapped around us, we dare,
To dream and live in the midnight air.

## Dreamy Nocturnal Whispers

In the quiet hours when all is still,
Whispers of dreams begin to thrill.
With every sigh, the night conspires,
To weave our thoughts into heart's desires.

Moonbeams trace the outlines of fate,
As shadows drift, we contemplate.
With each gentle rustle, hopes unfold,
In dreamy whispers, our stories told.

Through the darkness, a soft voice calls,
Echoes of love in the night's soft halls.
Wrapped in silence, we let go of fears,
Sharing our secrets, laughter, and tears.

As dawn approaches, painting the sky,
These nocturnal whispers will never die.
In every heartbeat, every shared glance,
We find our magic within this dance.

## Whispers of the Night Sky

In shadows deep, the secrets play,
The moonlight dances, dreams hold sway.
A breeze of whispers, soft and light,
Invites the heart to take its flight.

Stars twinkle bright, like scattered gems,
Each one a story, with timeless hems.
The night unfolds its velvet cloth,
A canvas where the dreams come froth.

Cool air wraps around, a gentle sigh,
Under the gaze of the vast, wide sky.
With every twinkle, a wish takes flight,
Carried along through the silent night.

In the stillness, hopes intertwine,
Lost in the echo, hearts align.
Embrace the magic that the night brings,
Awake to the wonder that dreaming sings.

## Lullabies Beneath the Stars

A soothing hum in the midnight breeze,
Sings lullabies among the trees.
Crickets chirp their gentle tune,
Under the watchful eye of the moon.

Beneath the stars, the world feels right,
Wrapped in dreams, embracing night.
Every twinkling spark a kiss,
Whispers of peace, a moment's bliss.

Waves of calm, like a gentle tide,
Cradling souls, in dreams they hide.
Time slows down, as hearts unwind,
In this realm, the world's unkind.

Close your eyes, let the shadows play,
Innocent wishes carried away.
With every breath, the stars align,
In lullabies, the heart will shine.

## Embrace of the Silver Glow

Silvery beams caress the ground,
Under this glow, calmness is found.
Night blooms softly, like a flower,
Each moment swells in this quiet hour.

The sky wears a cloak of twinkling light,
Guiding the lost through the tranquil night.
Embrace the silver that softly gleams,
A world reborn in whispered dreams.

As shadows dance, and starlight plays,
The heart finds peace in soft arrays.
Here in the silence, love speaks true,
In the embrace of the night, so new.

Glimmers of hope in every sigh,
Bathe in the beauty, let worries fly.
In this stillness, find what you seek,
In the silver glow, let the spirit speak.

## Serenade in Twilight

Twilight whispers as day departs,
Crafting a serenade for hearts.
Colors blend in a soft embrace,
Each moment held in a timeless space.

Birds sing low, their lullabies sweet,
Echoes of joy, a symphony neat.
The horizon blushes, as shadows grow,
A canvas painted in twilight's glow.

With every breath, the evening sighs,
Under the blanket of gathering skies.
Magic lingers, as night takes hold,
A serenade whispered, a story told.

Step into this world, let worries cease,
In twilight’s arms, discover peace.
Dance with the stars, let spirits ignite,
In the serenade of the coming night.

## Silhouettes in the Softest Glow

In twilight's hush, shadows align,
Whispers linger, soft and fine.
The world a canvas, painted light,
Where dreams unfurl, taking flight.

Silhouettes dance in twilight's grace,
Ethereal figures, time and space.
Each curve and edge, a silent song,
In the soft glow, we all belong.

Stars emerge, a distant choir,
Filling the night with their desire.
The breeze carries secrets low,
In the warmth of the softest glow.

With every sigh, the heart will know,
In silhouettes, we let love grow.
Time stands still, as shadows play,
In the night, we drift away.

## A Tapestry of Tranquil Dreams

In a world of whispers, soft and sweet,
Lies a tapestry beneath our feet.
Threads of silver, woven tight,
Creating visions that ignite.

Each dream a petal, gently spun,
In fields of stillness, we become one.
Colors blend in silent streams,
Framing our hearts with tranquil dreams.

Embrace the quiet, hold it near,
Let the calm dissolve all fear.
In this fabric, softly gleamed,
We find the peace we've always dreamed.

As night descends, the stars will gleam,
Mapping out our nightly dream.
A tapestry of love and light,
Guiding us into the night.

## Beneath the Gaze of a Gentle Moon

Beneath the gaze of silver light,
We wander softly through the night.
The moon whispers secrets, old and wise,
Casting shadows that mesmerize.

In fields of dreams, we softly roam,
Finding solace, far from home.
Each step a dance, a tender tune,
In the embrace of a gentle moon.

The stars are stitched in velvet skies,
Holding our hopes where silence lies.
In the cool air, our spirits swoon,
Lost in the gaze of the gentle moon.

Time pauses here, in stillness found,
Magic wraps the world around.
With every breath, a sweet commune,
Beneath the gaze of a gentle moon.

## Luella's Lullaby Beneath the Stars

Luella whispers in the night,
A lullaby, soft and light.
Stars twinkle down with gentle grace,
Bathing dreams in a warm embrace.

Her melody floats on a breeze,
Bringing calm with every tease.
A tender tune, for hearts to share,
Cradled softly in night’s sweet air.

Close your eyes, let visions gleam,
Find your peace, and sweetly dream.
With every note, a story flows,
Luella’s song, where love bestows.

Beneath the stars, the night is young,
A symphony of joy, unsung.
As dreams take flight, we're never far,
In Luella’s lullaby, beneath the stars.

## Tender Moments in Quietude

In the stillness of a gentle breeze,
Whispers dance among the leaves.
Hearts entwined in soft embrace,
Time suspends in this sacred space.

Beneath the glow of fading light,
We share secrets of the night.
The world outside fades and blurs,
While the silence softly stirs.

Caught in laughter, shadows play,
Every word a sweet ballet.
In tender moments, souls ignite,
As stars appear, we hold on tight.

Dreams unfurl like petals bright,
Painting visions in the night.
In quietude, we find our song,
Together here, we both belong.

## Silken Embrace Beneath the Stars

Underneath the velvet sky,
We weave our dreams as the night drifts by.
Each twinkle sings a tender tune,
In silken whispers, hearts commune.

The moonlight casts its silver glow,
Wrapping us in love's soft flow.
With every breath that we both share,
The universe feels our silent prayer.

Soft shadows play on the ground,
In this magic, we are unbound.
Stars above in quiet grace,
Reflect the light of your embrace.

Together here, lost in time,
In rhythm, our hearts softly chime.
In this stillness, we find our peace,
In silken dreams, our souls release.

## Harmonic Echoes in the Twilight

As daylight fades, the colors blend,
Hues of orange and purple send.
Echoes of laughter fill the air,
In twilight's arms, we gently stare.

The nightingale sings her sweet refrain,
In melodic harmony, love does reign.
Each note a brushstroke on the dark,
Creating light in every spark.

Familiar rhythms pulse and sway,
In twilight's light, we find our way.
With every heartbeat, we unite,
In sonic whispers of the night.

Time itself begins to glide,
In this moment, we're side by side.
Harmonic echoes softly play,
As twilight bids the world to stay.

## Cozy Reflections of the Dusk

In cozy corners, shadows blend,
The day behind us, it starts to end.
Candles flicker, casting glow,
In this warmth, our spirits flow.

A tapestry of memories unfolds,
As laughter wraps around us like gold.
With every glance, a story told,
In this sanctuary, we grow bold.

Time gently hushes, love's sweet muse,
In twilight’s grasp, we cannot lose.
Reflections linger as night takes hold,
In cozy whispers, our hearts unfold.

The dusk invites a calm embrace,
In shared moments, we find our place.
As stars awaken, dreams ignite,
In cozy reflections, all feels right.

## Shadows Dance on Satin Sheets

In the whisper of the night,
Shadows twirl with silent grace,
Satin glistens, pale moonlight,
Dreams weave through this sacred space.

Echoes of a distant sigh,
Breath of twilight, soft and slow,
Every heartbeat tells a lie,
In this dance, we ebb and flow.

Fingers trace a velvet line,
As the world fades into dark,
Time slows down, our souls entwine,
In this moment, we leave a mark.

With each flicker, shadows play,
A symphony of light and shade,
Lost in night, we drift away,
In this bed where dreams are made.

## Gentle Rhythms of the Evening

The sun dips low, a golden hue,
As evening whispers soft and low,
Waves of calm begin to strew,
In this twilight, hearts will glow.

Crickets sing their evening song,
While the stars begin to shine,
In the dark, we all belong,
To this moment, so divine.

Breezes carry scents so sweet,
Rustling leaves in tranquil dance,
Every heartbeat, every beat,
In this stillness, take a chance.

Underneath the velvet sky,
We find solace, hand in hand,
In these rhythms, we comply,
Letting go, as night is planned.

## Dreams Wrapped in Softest Light

Wrapped in hues of pale and gold,
Softest light begins to weave,
In the gentle night, we're told,
Every sigh is but a leave.

Clouds of cotton, soft and bright,
Cradle hopes and tender dreams,
In the hush of fading light,
Everything is as it seems.

Whispers of the moon’s embrace,
Lullabies for weary souls,
In this tranquil, sacred space,
Feel the magic, let it roll.

Every heartbeat shows the way,
Through the dark, we softly glide,
In the night, we choose to stay,
Holding dreams, our souls collide.

## Serenade of the Celestial Glow

Stars align in perfect song,
Every note a silver beam,
In this night where we belong,
Melodies flow like a dream.

Galaxies spin in slow dance,
Whispers of the cosmos call,
In this vast and endless expanse,
We find comfort, we stand tall.

Moonslight bathes us in its grace,
Softly guiding every thought,
In the dark, we find our place,
Life's true meaning, gently taught.

So we sway to celestial bliss,
Each twinkle tells a story,
In this serenade, we kiss,
Underneath the stars' old glory.

## Stardust and Soft Embraces

In twilight’s glow, we softly tread,
A dance of light, where dreams are spread.
With every breath, the cosmos sighs,
Stardust falls from velvet skies.

Whispers of love in a gentle breeze,
Embracing hearts, as time doth freeze.
Underneath the moon's sweet gaze,
We find our truth, in warmest ways.

Moments twinkle in night's embrace,
A quiet joy, a sacred space.
Hand in hand, we drift and sway,
In stardust fields, we'll forever play.

Together we'll weave the endless night,
Crafting dreams in the silver light.
With soft embraces, we'll always find,
The universe wrapped in heart and mind.

## Unraveled by the Night’s Melody

The night unfolds its velvet cloak,
With every note, a hidden hope.
Stars align, as shadows dance,
In harmony, we lose our chance.

A symphony of soft repose,
As whispers rise like blooming rose.
Each string, a heartbeat, softly sways,
Unraveled dreams in starry bays.

With every chord, a secret shared,
In music’s arms, we are ensnared.
The moonlight weaves a soothing spell,
In night's embrace, we lose ourselves.

As the echoes fade, the dawn appears,
We hold the night, through laughter and tears.
With every song that fills the sky,
Our spirits soar, forever high.

## A Harmonious Nest of Dreams

In gentle whispers, dreams take flight,
A nest of hope, beneath starlight.
Each feathered thought, a joy bestowed,
In harmony, our hearts explode.

Resting softly, we find our place,
Within the warmth of love’s embrace.
Beneath the canopy, wide and bright,
We gather wishes, taking flight.

With every heartbeat, a song is born,
A melody sung at the break of dawn.
In this nest, we find our peace,
Where all burdens fade and joys increase.

Together we dream, as shadows blend,
In this harmonious space, love won't end.
With every dawn, new songs we’ll weave,
In our nest of dreams, we shall believe.

## Celestial Comfort and Whispered Wishes

In the shimmering light of the night sky,
Whispered wishes begin to fly.
Stars twinkle softly, a celestial song,
In their embrace, we feel we belong.

Each wish unfurls like a bloom in spring,
Wrapped in comfort, our hearts take wing.
A tapestry woven with hopes and dreams,
Flowing gently in moonlit streams.

With every sigh, the cosmos hears,
A symphony built on laughter and tears.
Celestial beings watch and guide,
As we journey forth, with love as our light.

In this sacred space, we find our grace,
With whispered wishes, and time to chase.
Hearts entwined, we breathe as one,
In the warmth of the moon, our souls have spun.

## Silvery Serenity in the Stillness

The moonlight dances on the lake,
Whispers of stillness, softly awake.
Shadows stretch beneath the trees,
A gentle hush carried by the breeze.

Crickets sing their evening tune,
Stars emerge, a silvery boon.
Reflections flicker, spirits glide,
In nature's peace, we shall abide.

Quiet moments, hearts align,
Bathed in light, a life divine.
Every ripple tells a tale,
In silvery serenity, we sail.

With each breath, a soft embrace,
Lost in the night's serene grace.
Here beneath the vast expanse,
Silvery whispers invite us to dance.

## The Sweetness of Night's Caress

The night descends with a velvet cloak,
A lullaby wrapped in shadows' smoke.
Stars twinkle like jewels in the sky,
As dreams awaken, softly they sigh.

Moonbeams sprinkle the earth with light,
Kissing the world, a tender sight.
Night flowers bloom in fragrant air,
Every moment's a secret affair.

Whispers echo in the dark,
A sweet embrace, a tender spark.
Beneath the heavens, we find our place,
In the sweetness of night's warm grace.

Gentle waves of the night flow,
With every heartbeat, love does grow.
Wrapped in dreams, with spirits free,
We dance beneath the moonlit sea.

## The Gentle Calls of the Evening Veil

The sun dips low, shadows entwine,
In the evening's hush, all is fine.
A gentle breeze whispers our names,
As twilight settles, love reclaiming flames.

The sky transforms, a canvas bright,
Colors blend in soft twilight.
Birds return to nests up high,
As the stars awaken, one by one, they sigh.

Each call of crickets, a timeless song,
Guiding the weary back where they belong.
In the evening's veil, we find our peace,
A sacred space where all worries cease.

The world slows down, a tranquil pause,
With every heartbeat, we find our cause.
In whispers soft, the night reveals,
The gentle calls of the evening veils.

## Finding Refuge in the Stars Above

In the stillness of the night, we gaze,
Finding refuge in the cosmic haze.
Stars like lanterns in the sky,
Guide our dreams as they drift by.

The infinite stretches beyond our reach,
With every twinkle, the universe speaks.
Each shining light tells tales untold,
Of worlds unseen, and hearts of gold.

As we lay beneath this vast embrace,
Time stands still in this sacred place.
We breathe in wonder, eye to eye,
With galaxies swirling, they seem to sigh.

Finding refuge in the stars' sweet glow,
We become part of the celestial flow.
In the night's embrace, we find our way,
Carried gently until break of day.